# Saving Money Every Day

## A Woman's Guide To Living Frugally

**Marilyn Woodard**

ISBN-13:
978-1475108408

ISBN-10:
1475108400

Saving Money Every Day.

First Printing, 2012

Printed in the United States of America

# Table of Contents

# Authors Note

## OR, HOW TO READ THIS BOOK

Your best bet in reading this book is not to expect too much. Now, I don't mean that this book isn't great, because, of course it is. What I mean is, don't expect too much of *yourself*.

You see, some people read a book of tips and suggestions and think it is a book of commands. And when it turns out that they can't perform all the commands, they think they've failed. They get all overwhelmed and think, "I'll never be able to do all that!"

<u>Tip</u>: **No one is expecting you to**
**act on every single idea in this book.**

Say you get all freaked out at the thought of tracking all your spending. That's okay. It's just a sign you aren't ready for that yet. But maybe you find three new ideas for saving money. Consider yourself successful!

Now, I do hope that when those three ideas are a regular part of your life, you'll come back and visit this book again. Who knows? This time you may be ready to make some changes in your credit card habits. At the very least, you might find another Mind Game that will help you stash away some savings.

Remember

Every little positive change is a win!

# Introduction

Saving money: everyone wants to do it. We all know we need to do it. But somehow there never seems to be any extra money to save. Sound familiar? It should, because you are not alone.

In a poll of Americans of working age, 75% said they knew that their savings, targeted for retirement, were insufficient.

If you are reading this book, you are probably in that 75 percent, or are afraid you are, or are trying to figure out how not to be. Good for you! Here's some good news for you.

### How much you save has very little to do with how rich you are.

Surprised? It's true. A recent study by Venti and Wise, *"Choice, Chance and Wealth Dispersion at Retirement,"* found that lower-income earners, on average, save more than middle-income earners – some by as much as $100,000! This is remarkable when you think about it. Those with less saved more!

This is **Good News** for you! It means that *anyone* can save money. All you have to do is learn what those lower-income savers know. And you've come to the right book to learn it.

# A New Mindset

A "new mindset" means changing the way you think about money. You may be doing fine on a week-to-week basis. You may think you just want to have a little extra spending money. Or you may be in a real money crunch; in debt and going under fast. You may be able to work for that extra money for Christmas. You can even get out of a financial crisis without a real change in your thinking. But, if you do not change your thoughts, you are guaranteeing that you will be right back in the same situation; probably sooner rather than later.

You probably feel at a loss as to how you will come up with extra money. You are barely eking out a living now. But, you can do it if you train yourself to think differently. When you train your brain to think frugally and creatively about money, you will become more prosperous.

## *Small Changes, Big Results*

The great Albert Einstein once said,

**"It takes a genius to see the obvious."**

Sometimes the simpler things in life are the most powerful. Because they are so obvious we tend to ignore them and not let them work for us.

# The Magic Notebook

One of the most powerful mindset changing ideas you can adopt is this: keep a daily diary of what you spend. Go to the dollar store, buy a little book, and carry it with you wherever you go. Write down every penny – each single penny - you spend. If you do this one thing, you will find that something magical happens in your financial life in a matter of weeks.

Writing down each of your expenditures makes the flow of money through your life more real to you. It shows you simply and clearly just exactly where - and on what - you are spending your money. Once you know this, it becomes much easier to control your spending.

**Example:** Marie stops in at a coffee shop before work every day. She saves money by ordering a two-dollar plain coffee instead of a latte. And she has the two-dollar pastry instead of the four-dollar breakfast sandwich.

She only buys the latte on Saturdays on her way home from her workout. A girl deserves a treat then, right?

But then, Marie starts writing down her expenses...

She sees that four dollars shows up six days a week. She does a little simple math.

**$ 4 Dollars**
**x 6 Days a week**

**$24 Dollars**

**$ 24 Dollars**
**x 52 Weeks a year**
**$1,248 Dollars!**

Marie hasn't had a vacation in years. She suddenly realizes that by giving up coffee and pastry she can take her children on vacation next year. Even if she only gives up the pastry she could make next Christmas look a lot merrier!

# *E-Z Step One*

Go buy a small notebook today! Better yet, scrounge around. The perfect notebook could be languishing in your kid's bottom drawer. You might even enjoy sporting a Hello Kitty notebook!

**There may be nothing but a**
**75-cent notebook and a ballpoint pen**
**between financial struggle**
**and financial freedom.**

## *Spending for Real Needs*

Before you can even begin, you have to say no to excess spending. You have start spending for real needs, not for fun, or comfort, or your self-esteem.

Real fun and comfort can be found for free and will not leave you feeling guilty or panicked about unpaid bills. If your self-esteem needs a boost, think about what a responsible person you are becoming. Be proud of the fact that you can take care of yourself and your family.

Perhaps you need to spend some time thinking about this question: *"What is enough?"* Answering that question in your own terms can bring peace of mind, focus and determination to your plans and actions.

**Exchange shopping time for something better.** Notice I said "exchange," not, "give up." Your brain does not like a void. So if you just give up shopping, your brain will not let you stop thinking about it. Your brain will *demand* that you take it shopping. But, if you fill up the shopping void with something better, your brain may whimper, but it will get over it. And soon, it will accept the change and *prefer* the new activity.

Go for a walk, take the kids to the park, dust off that old guitar and start practicing. Anything you'd like to do, or think you should do, that you "don't have time for," will give you more long-term satisfaction than buying a new trinket.

## *Learn From Others*

You have friends and

relatives whom you have always thought of as "cheap" or "tightwads." It's time to start thinking of them as "smart!" Watch what they do and then copy their tight-fisted ways.

Use it up,
Wear it out,
Make it do,
Do without.

Did your grandmother save aluminum foil and re-use it? If you thought that was quaint, think again. Every piece of foil she re-used was a piece she didn't have to buy.

Do you have a friend who doesn't earn a lot but always manages to take a vacation? Ask her how she does it.

**Spend time with your frugal friends.** Just being around them will encourage you in your new mindset. They will understand what you are trying to achieve. They will accept your new behavior and cheer you on.

Be prepared to lose touch with your free-spending friends. They might say, "Good for you!" but, when you stop going to the mall and can't join them for dinner very often, they may stop calling. Don't take it personally. They just can't think of anything else to do with their time.

Read books about money, especially this one! You will find the financial wisdom of generations of money smart people in these pages. Putting just a few of these ideas to work will make a big difference in your bottom line.

Wait a few months and read it again. You will find ideas you missed the first time and a few more tricks you can easily work into your lifestyle. Repeat at least once a year.

# Become Inspired

Before you decide your shirt is out of style and you must buy another one, ask your frugal fashionista friend how you can restyle it and wear it another year.

Learn a new skill. There are books and videos on just about any topic at your local library. If you have an Internet connection there is a world of knowledge at your fingertips: and most of it is on YouTube!

Spend your spare time online and search out those frugal Web sites. Look at "living cheaply," "frugal living" and "simple lifestyle." You'll find a ton of good Web sites devoted to living on less.

# Positive Thinking and Visualization

Positive thinking and visualization are two key concepts used by people who are mildly to wildly successful in any field you care to name. The power of positive and negative thoughts has been recognized for centuries. The book of Psalms (ca. 2000 BC) says, "As a man thinks in his heart, so is he." Your thinking determines, not only your behavior, but who you are becoming.

## Brain Changing Tips

**How can I?** The next time you say, "I can't do..," stop and restate it as a question. When you state something as a negative, your brain believes you. It will continue to work on that basis and what you have said will become true. You have essentially put up a big Stop sign for your brain. By turning it into a question, you leave your brain free to work on the answer.

**Example:**
**"I can't save money."**

**Change to,**
**"How can I save money?"**

You will be amazed at the new, innovative ideas you see and hear around you. Your brain may even come up with something out of "nowhere!"

**What if?** Do you hear yourself saying things like, "I never win anything," or, "Nothing good ever happens to me."? Turn your brain loose by asking the question, "What if?"
**"What if I win this time?"**
**"What if this turns out to be a great day?"**

Saying these things to yourself will feel very awkward at first. Keep it up anyway. Keep it up until it feels normal. I guarantee that, at the very least, you will have a more cheerful outlook.

*Visualization*

Joe is giving you directions to his house. As he talks you see in your mind's eye the school on the corner where you turn right, the park on the left that is just before the traffic circle where you have to go around the circle to turn left. Your brain is automatically visualizing something it has never seen or done before. This is how your brain helps you succeed at a new task.

Visualization is just intentionally using your brain's normal technique to help you succeed. Athlete's use it to

17

mentally practice perfect moves when they are injured, or just sitting still. When they get back to practicing physically, their mind has been working in the background to turn the images into reality.

You can use this technique to realize your dream of wise spending, finding bargains and building your savings

# E-Z Step Two

Spend a little time every day "seeing" yourself accomplishing your goals. See yourself smiling as you pay *all* the bills for the month. See yourself putting $100 in a savings account. Then trust your brain to help you turn that dream into reality.

# Time to Crunch some Numbers

## *But, but, but…*

Do you feel overwhelmed, reluctant, maybe even scared at the thought of getting your finances on paper? That's okay! Pretty much everyone does.

The reason you are reading this book is that you no longer want to live like pretty much everyone. You want much more than that. You knew it wouldn't be easy. Easy is what got you where you are now.

But it is not as hard as you think it is. It is your emotions that are holding you back. Remember this: It is just a task. You do not have to give in to your emotions about the task. After all, as a mother you do all kinds of nasty things just because they need to be done. This job doesn't even require holding your nose!

## *Getting Down To It*

Here's the deal. You can't fix the problem without a clear idea of what the problem is!

If you are like most people, you don't know enough about your own financial reality. If you've had more than one job this year, you might not even know what you've earned. Do you know what it takes to live comfortably, how much your discretionary income is, and the exact amount of your debt?

**Why is it important to know this stuff?** Two reasons:

**First,** you need to know exactly how much you owe, how much money you have in hand, and what it will take to cover the distance between the two.

**Second,** Knowing will help you avoid setbacks such as penalties, further repairs, missed deadlines, etc.

Whether on your own, with a financial counselor*, or using an online tool (see Resources,) your first step is to assess the situation.

Once you know how much money you have and how much money you truly need, you can make realistic plans.

*Don't immediately rule out the idea of paying someone to help you do this. Make sure they will charge you a set fee for a certain amount of time, or for a certain service. Have all your paperwork rounded up and organized and take it with you. It may be the best $100 or $200 you ever spent.

# Saving Money or

# Spending Less?

You decide you truly need new shoes for work. This is a genuine need so you gird up your loins, take cash in hand and prepare to find a bargain.

Three stores and many, many horribly expensive shoes later you find them. They fit, they are the right color, they suit your needs perfectly and...*they are 50% off!* You can't wait to tell the ladies at work how much money you saved.

Wait. Did you save money? Or did you just spend less than the retail price?

If you are really going to save money you need to take the amount you did not have to hand over to the sales clerk and actually put it in your savings account.

Think about it. If you spent $30 on those shoes instead of the $60 they cost at the other stores, what will happen to the $30 you "saved?"

It's going to be spent on something else, that's what. Or, you could deposit it in your savings account on the way home from the store. And it will sit there earning interest until you truly need it.

As Benjamin Franklin said,

A penny
saved
is a penny
earned.

## *E-Z Step Three*

On a business sized envelope write, "Savings." Put that envelope in your purse. When you save money on a purchase, put the amount saved in the envelope. Drop by your bank as soon as you can and deposit the cash in your savings account.

# Saving Money and Credit Cards

Experts tell us the average American is holding around $8,000 in credit card debt. It doesn't take an expert to know why. It's because paying with a little piece of plastic is easy!

When you pay with cold hard cash, you *see* your supply of money shrinking. When you write a check you see the numbers growing smaller. That fact alone will make you think twice about how badly you need a new DVD or those fabulous new shoes.

## *Ban Credit Cards*

A very good rule of thumb is, unless you pay off your credit card bills each month, don't use them! Nothing encourages thriftiness like having to pay cash for everything.

You probably get at least one new credit card offer in the mail each week. Make it a habit to throw them away without opening them. (Tear the whole thing in half before throwing it away to insure no one else uses the form, and your name and address, to apply for the card.)

**The only exception** to the throw-'em-away rule is if you get an offer of an extremely low rate of interest on transferred balances. If you already have several credit cards, each at different rates of interest, take advantage of the offer to fold them into one low-interest account.

Usually you will have 6 months to a year with no or low interest. Do your darnedest to pay off the balance before the interest rate goes up. And *pay attention* to that interest rate once the time runs out on the low rate! You could save hundreds this way.

**Compare Offers.** Get out the calculator! Depending on how much you owe and how much you can pay each month, a card with 2% interest for twelve months may work better for you than a card with 1.5% for six months.

**Take Notice!** This new low-interest card is NOT for making new purchases. There is a different, *and higher*, rate of interest for new purchases!

## *The Credit Card as a Tool*

Perhaps you can't imagine life without any credit cards at all. It is true that many financially savvy people use a credit card as a tool. Some people use a credit card for gasoline purchases only. Others use a credit card when travelling so they don't have to carry large amounts of cash. Online purchases require a credit card or an online payment service like PayPal. For those who can use it in a disciplined way, this is all fine.

But, be honest with yourself. If you have a credit card, will you be tempted to buy things you don't need? If the answer is yes, you'd better stick with cash only.

24

## Credit Card Fees

Credit cards are just about the most expensive form of money. Not only do you pay interest on any amount that is not paid in-full and on-time, there are other fees to consider.

- **Annual Fee**. This is what you pay for the privilege of using the card. That's right. Even if you don't use it, you are paying for the right to use it. Cards that offer a lot of bells and whistles – rewards, cash back, a concierge service – tend to have higher annual fees. A card with no extra benefits should have a lower annual fee. (Though there are no guarantees. You have to read the fine print!)

- **Late Fee.** It doesn't matter how small the amount you owe. It doesn't matter if you have paid your bill in full every month for years. If your check arrives one day late, you will pay the full late fee. It is entirely possible to owe $4.47 for a shirt you bought on clearance and end up paying a $35.00 late fee. Ouch!

- 

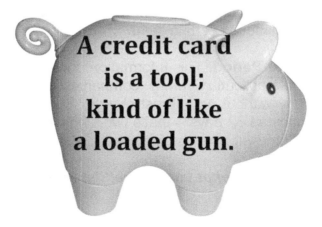

A credit card
is a tool;
kind of like
a loaded gun.

**Over-the-Limit Fee.** Some cards will not allow you to spend more than the stated limit. If you try, your card will be rejected. However, some will let you keep on spending and then charge you another fee for that "privilege."

**Remember, a credit card is a
cash-management tool,
NOT a borrowing tool.**

# Credit Card Offers

You've decided you have the moxie to handle a credit card. Which one should you get? First, check the information given above under the subtitle, "Fees."

**Rewards Cards.** Find a card that rewards you with cash. You want a credit on your account or a check in the mail, *not* a catalog of available products. A new coffee maker is fine, but not when you need new shoes. With cash, you can choose your own products.

**Compare rewards programs.** One may give you one point for every dollar you spend and then require that you spend $10,000 to earn a reward. Another may require a lower number of points to earn a reward, but only reward you for purchases of certain items.

**Interest-Free Period.** This information should be on the credit card application. Many companies give you 55 days to pay without an interest charge. Some may give you as many as 62 days – that's two whole months! But, look out! Some will give you far less.

*Know what you are getting into.*

# *E-Z Step 4*

Find your credit card statement. Find the section that says "Payment Information," or words to that effect. It should be on the first page and/or with the Statement Summary. This will tell you, *in dollars and cents,* exactly how much it costs when you do not pay off your bill.

# Saving Money Every Day...

There are lots of ways to save money. From playing tricks on yourself to plugging energy leaks in your house, there is always another tip to try.

Read through all of the tips and check the ones that are one-time tasks. These are the easiest tips: do them once and forget them.

The tricks that ask you to change your behavior are another story. Breaking a habit, or creating a new one, is all about training your brain to work in a new way. Psychologists have established that it takes 28 days, about a month, to establish new thought patterns.

Overloading your brain with 47 new behaviors at once is not nice. Be kind to your brain and expect it to work on one or two new things at a time. Your brain will, in turn, help you to save money every day.

**Enjoy Life!**
**When you save your first**
**$100 or pay off a debt, grab**
**the kids and dance, have fun,**
**hold a ceremony, make a**
**memory.**

This list is organized by categories which are listed alphabetically. Try one or two tips at a time. Do the ones that seem easiest for you. Later, come back and revisit a category or two and try a couple more tips.

Relax and get ready to start saving money every day.

## *With Mind Games*

**Give yourself a weekly allowance.** Put a set amount of spending money into an envelope. Use it for your incidental spending: a needed cup of java or an emergency meal when your schedule collapses. The trick is, when the money is gone, you don't get any more until next week.

**Have your paycheck automatically deposited** directly to your savings account. Then transfer bill-paying money to your checking account and take out enough cash to cover your groceries and incidentals for the week. Think twice about withdrawing any more.

**Play the Don't-Break-a-Ten Game**. Establish one envelope to stash one-dollar bills. Try to spend these before you break a larger bill. If something costs$12.00, pay with a ten and two ones rather than handing over two tens, or even a ten and a five. This helps your mind to work on saving larger bills. Any large bills left at the end of the week go into savings.

**Put your change in the piggy bank.** Always give the cashier whole dollars, not the exact amount. In a few months, you will have "found" money for savings.

> You'll have to put the coins in rolls in order to deposit them in the bank. The bank will be happy to give you the paper rolls, and you

29

can fill them up while watching TV or having a conversation.

**Toss the Wish Books.** We used to call the Sears Catalog the "Wish Book." If you have "wish books" from department stores, jewelry stores, book clubs, tool stores, or whatever tempts you, Throw Them Out!

There is an exception here. If there is something that will motivate you to save money (a new TV or a vacation spot) cut out a picture of it and put it where you can see it every day.

## At Your Bank

**Shop for a bank** by comparing their fees and services.

- Do they charge for ATM withdrawals?

- What is their overdraft (bounced check) policy? Look for a bank with the lowest penalties and the most service.

- Are they charging a fee for your checking account, or your savings account?

- Do you have to keep a large balance in order to have a free checking account? Find a bank that will give you a free account with a low balance and keep the larger amount in an interest-bearing savings account.

**Enter and deduct all checks and debits** in your check register as soon as possible. It's very easy to run out of money without realizing it.

**Pad your checking account** with an extra $50 or $100 that you **do not** enter in your check register. It will help you avoid a bounced check should you make a mistake in your subtraction.

## *On Beauty*

**Simplify your hairstyle**. If it is simple enough you may be able to get it cut by a friend or go to one of the cheap chain salons.

Anything that requires chemicals is very expensive in a salon. Products for coloring or perming your hair at home are very good and are available at your supermarket. If you are skittish, ask a friend who does her own hair to help you choose and use the right product. You will probably be pleasantly surprised by how well your hair turns out.

Longer hair can go longer between cuts.

**Use a bath sponge or puff** with only one pump of liquid soap. Train everyone in the family to do this. They will have more than enough suds for a shower.

**Dilute liquid soaps and shampoos**. Start with ¼ water to ¾ soap and adjust to your liking.

**Take care of your own nails.** Expensive manicures are for very rich, or very poor, people. This is a skill, not an art. You can learn to do it.

**Buy inexpensive, drugstore cosmetics.** Compare active ingredients listed on the label. If they are the same, the product will work as well as the celebrity-endorsed brand.

If you cannot bear to do without your department store makeup, at least buy them when they offer a gift with purchase. These make great Christmas gifts!

## *On Your Car*

**Save hundreds on towing** by keeping some basic supplies in your trunk – and learning to use them!

### *Checklist for Car Emergencies*

Jack & lug wrench
Spare tire
Shovel – for digging out of snow or mud
Battery jumper cables
Basic tool kit
Fix-A-Flat Kit
Oil
Air pump that plugs into the lighter
Gallon of drinking water
Blankets
Basic first aid kit
Flashlight with extra batteries
Emergency food
Candles and matches
Map
Cell phone or C.B. can literally be a life saver

**Look into your interest rate.** Are you making payments on your car? If rates have fallen significantly since you bought the car, see if you can refinance.

**Shop for insurance every year.** As always, ask, "Is this the best you can do?"

**Keep up on regular maintenance.** This can prevent big repair bills.

Regular maintenance will also make your car last longer. You may even double the life of your car. That saves the cost of a new car!

**Learn to change the oil and filters in your car.** There is a how-to video available on YouTube.com for just about any make and model.

**Treat your car gently.** Accelerate slowly, brake gently, corner with all four wheels on the ground! You may not look as cool when you drive, but you'll appreciate not replacing tires, brakes, belts and gasoline as often as your "cooler" friends do.

**Bus it to work.** If you live in an area that has public transportation, see how much you can save by taking a bus or train to work every day. Or, ride your bike to work in good weather.

**Put your kids on the school bus** rather than driving them to school.

## Looking for a new car?

**Research Prices.** CarTalk.com is a good resource. Or, as with any research project, ask your local librarian.

**Buy Used.** Think about getting a new-to-you car. The up-front cost is lower, so are insurance rates.

**Buy from an owner** rather than a dealer. The owner gets more for his car than he would by trading it in. You pay less than you would at a dealer. (Remember, you will still have to pay sales tax when you register the car.)

## On Gasoline

**Get a gasoline credit card** *if you can pay it off each month*. Some gas stations offer pretty significant savings on gas when you use their card.

**Use the cheaper gasoline.** Car makers assume buyers will use the cheap stuff so they design the engines accordingly.

**Check the Internet**. Search for "cheap gas" to find web sites that show you the best deals in your area.

**Pay attention to price change timing.** In our area, the lowest price of the week is usually on Thursday. It jumps for the weekend when people are more likely to be out and about.

**Don't fill the tank when prices are higher.** Gas prices are subject to many forces (I think mirrors and genies are involved,) but a major force is supply and demand. When the price rises too high, people stop buying. That's lower demand, which causes greater supply, which causes lower prices. So buy a few gallons to get you by, and fill up when the price drops.

**Don't drive when you don't absolutely have to**. Bundle your shopping and errands into one trip. You really don't have to jump in the car just because you ran out of milk. Your kids will live a couple of days without it.

**Drive at a consistent speed.** Use cruise control when you can. You'll use less gas than when you speed up and slow down, even a little.

**Clean out your car.** If you have heavy objects in your car that you don't need, remove them. It takes more fuel to move a heavier vehicle.

**Avoid letting your car idle.** If you are going to be stopped for more than one minute, save gas by turning the car off.

**Give your car a good tune up.** While giving your car a tune up won't actually save you money at the pump, it will save gas. Using less gas saves you money.

**Are you considering a hybrid?** Hybrids are more expensive than regular cars, and the savings in gas will not pay for the difference overnight. In fact, it may take years for the gasoline savings to equal the extra you paid for the car. However, federal and state governments may offer tax breaks for hybrid owners. Then too, as gasoline prices rise, these cars will make more economic sense.

**Check the tire air pressures weekly.** Buy an inexpensive manual air pump and an accurate tire gauge (not a pencil gauge as they are not accurate). Keep all tires inflated to the same pressure as recommended for your car but not for your tire. Go by the sticker on the doorframe and not the tire wall.

## *With Your Credit Card*

**Subtract your credit card purchases immediately** from your checking account so you're not surprised once the bill arrives.

You might even write out a check to "Cash." When it's time to pay the credit card bill, deposit all checks made out to "Cash" in your checking account. Then write your check to the credit card company.

**Check your interest rate.** Right now. Find out how much your credit card company is charging you in interest. Then shop for a card with a lower rate. If you are the "Average American" with over $8,000 in credit card debt, and you lower your interest rate by 2-3%, you will save thousands of dollars in interest fees.

## On Your Checking and Debit Card

*Always, always, always* **subtract** debit card purchases from your check register.

**Put $100 in your checking account but,** *do not enter it in the check register.* Now you have a cushion against overdrafts. (Also known as bounced checks!) When the numbers in the checkbook get down to single digits, you stop spending. After a while you may even forget you have the cushion. This is a Good Thing!

## On Clothes

**Shop at consignment stores and thrift shops.** Look for gently worn, or even new, clothes for 1/10 the price of new.

You won't find as much for grade school children at thrift or consignment shops. The reason? They wear out their clothes! Still, if you are looking for dressier clothes, thrifty is the way to go.

**Mend your clothing** instead of buying new clothes. This is a skill, not an art. It can be learned and perfected through practice.

**Shop in the yard.** Look for quality, name brand clothing at yard and garage sales in more affluent neighborhoods.

**Shop 50% off the clearance price.** This is my favorite way to shop in department stores. They have brand new clothes at thrift store prices. Sure, they are end-of-the-season leftovers, but don't turn up your nose until you check them out.

**Buy neutral basics:** shirts, skirts and pants that will last several seasons. Add color and trendiness with accessories.

**No dry cleaning allowed!**

Most clothes that have a "Dry Clean Only" label can be hand washed in cold water. When in doubt, check with Martha Stewart (see Resources.) She really does know everything.

I bought a silk blouse for $7. What a buy! Then I took it to be dry cleaned and shelled out $15. Ouch!

A home dry-cleaning kit that works in the dryer can clean several garments for around $10.

## On Doctor Bills

**Quit smoking.** You know what you will save in cigarette costs. Just think of the boatloads of money and trouble you will save in the future by *not* having to deal with emphysema or lung cancer.

**Exercise.** You don't have to go from couch potato to marathon runner. Even 15 minutes of daily walking makes a positive difference in your health.

**Brush and floss your teeth daily** to keep the dentist bill down. The flossing is important. Most serious dental problems begin with the gums and can be avoided by regular flossing.

**Eat real food.** Invest some time in learning to cook whole foods. Your body will respond favorably to the lack of preservatives, monosodium glutamate, and artificial colorings.

An apple a day keeps the doctor away.

**Buy generic** over-the-counter medicine rather than name brand items when possible. The law says they have to contain the same amount of the same active ingredients.

**Learn basic First Aid.** Knowledge of first aid and some basic supplies can save a trip to the doctor, or even the emergency room.

### *Suggestions for a Home Medical Kit*

First Aid Book - get a newer edition, make sure it is well illustrated and is easy to understand.
Home Remedies book
Thermometer
Cold medicines
Cough medicines
Cough drops/throat discs
Eyewash
Pain relief medicine (acetaminophen)
Anti-inflammatory medication (aspirin or ibuprofen)
Antibiotic and Antifungal Ointments
Pure Aloe Vera gel - good for minor burns, cuts, scrapes
Burn treatment, such as Water Jel
Hydrogen Peroxide for cleansing wounds
Isopropyl Alcohol for sterilizing skin and/or instruments
Cotton for applying alcohol, etc.
Diarrhea medication
Oral electrolytes such as Gator Ade (for dehydration from fever, diarrhea, stress)
Tweezers
Needles to remove slivers
Bulb syringe for cleaning ears
Bandages in several sizes for small cuts and abrasions
For larger wounds:
Gauze pads
Surgical tape or Paper tape
Scissors
Hemostats for clamping a blood vessel
Dental kit to patch dentures or a tooth with a lost filling
Oral pain relief gel

## If you do not have health insurance:

1. Talk to the doctor and/or his bookkeeper. They may be willing to lower their fees considerably. Health insurance companies *never* pay the full price. (ASK: "Is that the best you can do?)

2. They will probably be willing to accept payments, instead of requiring the whole fee up front. Remind them that, even if it takes several months to pay your bill, they will still be getting their money sooner than if they were being paid by an insurance company.

## *On Energy*

You already know your energy bill eats up a big chunk of your monthly income. Traditionally it ranks third, behind housing and food. Recently, it seems  to be trying to move into second, or even first place! Now is the time to use every trick in the book to cut energy costs.

**Switch to compact fluorescent light bulbs.** They are expensive to buy, but their longer life and lower energy consumption offset that cost. They use about 80-90% less energy than standard bulbs.

**Turn off and unplug appliances** when not in use, especially if you are leaving for a few days. Do you really need the clock on the coffee maker and microwave to be running while you're gone?

**Turn off the hot water heater.** Don't panic! I mean, when you are gone for a few days it does not need to be heating water. It only takes a few hours to heat up once you turn it back on.

**Try to keep your freezer full**. It takes less energy to keep things cold than to keep airspace cold. If you are running low on food, you can fill up the space with clean old milk bottles filled with water.

**Defrost your freezer *quickly*.** Remove the food; pack it closely in a cooler (or a cardboard box using newspapers for insulation.) Turn the freezer off, open it and place a fan where it will blow directly into the freezer. Within 10 to 15 minutes you should be able to remove large chunks of ice from the walls of the freezer. Mop up the remaining water and let the fan do the final drying. You should be able to turn the freezer back on – and pop your still frozen food back in - within 30-45 minutes of the time you turned it off.

## On Entertainment

**Do have the occasional movie or dinner out.** Keep working toward your financial goals. But realize that all humans need a little fun once in a while. Live is too short to pinch pennies all day, everywhere, all the time.

**Cancel subscriptions** to magazines and newspapers you don't need. Read magazine subscriptions at the library or buy them at the thrift shop for 25 to 50 cents after someone else has read them.

**Read all the books you want for free.** Borrow them from the library.

**If you must own books** (and some of us *must*) check thrift stores and garage sales.

**Make it at home.** Do you stop for a morning cup of coffee on your way to work? Set it up the night before and save dollars a day.

**Watch it on DVD.** The next time you yearn to see a movie, wait to see it on DVD. Rent it at the video store. Better yet, borrow it from the library. (You may be able to request that the library buy a movie you want to see.)

**Get social.** Organize a movie and book swap party. Everyone off-loads the ones they've lost interest in and goes home with something new.

**Do an un-restaurant.** A pot-luck dinner, or a more formally arranged dinner club, is a great alternative to eating out with friends. Everyone gets to show off what they brought, the different dishes are conversation starters, and everyone gets to try new things.

**Keep a sharp eye out.** Compete with your kids, spouse, or just try to top your Personal Best by seeing how many coins you can find on the ground when you are out and about.

## On Gifts

**Think Christmas all year long.** When you see a great gift at a great price, grab it and stash it away. Just be sure to keep track of them. You want to remember where they are come December! And, of course, you don't want to have five gifts for your daughter and one for your son.

**Yes, it is all right to re-gift!** If it's something common, like a bottle of wine or a box of chocolates, you are very safe. If it's Aunt Martha's hand crocheted tissue box cover, make sure you give it to someone Aunt Martha will *never* meet!


## *On Home Furnishings*

**De-store it.** Do you have "stuff" in a storage unit? Have you used any of that stuff in the last six months? If not, it's time to clear it out. If you haven't used it in six months to a year, why are you spending money on it? Hold a garage sale, invite family and friends to come take what they want, and donate the rest. Then use that rental money to make your life better.

**Slipcover or reupholster** your old furniture. There is no magic involved in these jobs. They are skills you can learn as you do them. (Start with the back!) Again, YouTube is a great educational resource.

**Refinish or paint** wood or plastic furniture. There are amazing new paint products that allow you to paint almost anything. And almost anyone can get a pretty good looking finish with spray paint.

**Buy used.** Beautiful furniture, artwork, and linens are all out there waiting for you to get over the mystique of "new." Goodwill, other thrift shops, and consignment shops offer a huge opportunity to have beautiful furnishings at low cost. Some may need a little refurbishing, but many are perfect.

**Think outside the box** and create a unique and beautiful environment that doesn't look like anyone else's. Get ideas from design books, television shows and blogs. See Resources.

Jan needed a sofa.
Budget: $300.
She found exactly what she wanted.
Retail cost: $1,500.
Consignment store cost: $300.

## *With Homemaking*

**Re-use grocery bags.** The plastic ones make great trash bags.

**Use generic cleaning products** rather than name-brand. Even if you use a coupon, the name-brand costs more.

**Make your own** window cleaner, laundry soap, etc. Recipes for these products can be found online. Good resources include eHow.com and Tipnut.com.

**Invest in cloth.** For napkins, check estate sales and Goodwill. They won't make much of an impact on your laundry and you save on paper. The same goes for cleaning cloths. A stack of old washcloths or hand towels is a great substitute for paper towels.

## On Your House

**Do a yearly energy check.** Replace all essentials, such as cracked storm windows, and worn out weather stripping. All kinds of repair jobs can be done by the average person. Books and videos are good places to learn. Make your motto: "Done is better than perfect."

**Never be afraid** to learn from your friends and neighbors. Chances are they'll enjoy sharing their skills with you. From gardening to replacing a doorknob to a full-scale remodel, the people in your life are often happy to help.

**Feed them, heap on the praise,
and return the favor. You'll gain much more
than the cost of the repair.**

**Are you renting?**

**Ask for a break.** Are you a good renter, i.e., you keep the lawn mowed, are respectful of the property and your neighbors? Before you move to save on rent, try calling the landlord. Tell him you like the house but are thinking of moving to save money. Ask if he will lower the rent to keep you there. A smart landlord knows that good renter saves him money, so he might cut you a deal. Even if it's only for a few months, that little extra can help you pay off other bills or go into your savings account.

## Are you buying your home?

**Check rates.** When mortgage rates are especially low, look into refinancing your mortgage. You may be able to save thousands in interest.

### Private Mortgage Insurance, or PMI:

Every mortgage requires you to carry this and the cost is included in your mortgage payment. If you received, or refinanced, your loan **after July 29, 1999** there is good news. Your lender is required to drop your PMI once your equity is over 22% (assuming you have a good payment history.) However, if your mortgage began before that date, you could still be paying for unnecessary insurance. Check into it right away.

If you find you have been paying for PMI, you may suddenly have a substantial amount of money *not* eaten up by your mortgage. You have some choices.

1. You could keep paying that amount to your mortgage, thereby paying off the mortgage much earlier. This could save you thousands of dollars. Your lender can tell you exactly how much.

2. You could add that amount to your 401(k). If your employer matches that amount your retirement savings will be exceptional. You really cannot have too much money for retirement.

3. You could add that amount to your conventional savings, update your house, or help pay for your children's college tuition.

4. You could use some of the money in each of these areas.

5. You could just add it to the household budget and raise your immediate standard of living. If you choose this option, you have not been paying attention.

**If you are in the market for a house:**

- Look at foreclosed property. A bank owns the house. If it's been on their books for a while, or if they have a lot of houses on their books, they may be willing to give you a steep discount.

- Think pre-foreclosure homes. Ask around, tell everyone and anyone what you are looking for and that you are willing to buy a home from someone who would otherwise have to go through foreclosure. If you can buy them out for the amount left on their mortgage, you are doing them a huge favor. It's a win-win situation.

- Look for rent-to-own property. Usually you will have no realtor's fee and no huge deposit. The owner is willing to do this because, if you stop paying, he gets the house back. At the same time, you are creating equity and have pride of ownership.

## *On Your Wonderful Children*

**Breastfeed your babies.** Not only do you save money on formula, it's good for your health and good for the baby's health. And there is no better way to bond with your infant.

**Buy generic** baby wipes, diapers, and formula. Compare the ingredient labels and you'll see that they have the same ingredients.

47

**Make your own.** Better yet, Google "homemade baby wipes." You'll find a gaggle of recipes.

**Never say no** to hand-me-downs. From clothing to bikes to textbooks, these are wonderful gifts.

**Kids' Allowance.**

This may be even more controversial than breastfeeding! But, giving your children an allowance is not mandatory. When they are too young to work, they really don't need money. If they perceive the need for money, help them find creative ways to save on their own. Maybe they can do chores for friends, neighbors or relatives. Maybe they can collect aluminum cans. They can ask for cash instead of toys for birthdays and Christmas. Not only will your kids be learning about economics, they will gain confidence and satisfaction from earning what they want.

**The "cool" factor:** your older kids may want clothes with whatever label is currently considered fashionable. Give them choices. Tell them how much you can spend and let them decide how to spend it. They will learn a lot from the experience.

**Do not worry** if your child doesn't have a lot of toys, or the more expensive toys. Help her to be creative and make her own toys. Give him a cardboard box and see what fun he has with it. Rocks, sticks, mud and "let's pretend" are still some of the best toys available.

I gave my 12-year old a choice: one pair of cool jeans or three pair of store brand jeans. He chose cool. His fifth-grade teacher saw them every day but, he was happy!

# In The Kitchen

**Plan your meals** a week (or more) at a time. Then make out your grocery list. You will save money by not buying on impulse. You will save money by not eating out. You will save a lot of stress by not having to think about dinner at the last minute.

**Do buy some convenience items.** On those days when you get home late, are sick, or just plain too tired to cook, a tray of frozen lasagna will feed the family for far less than a delivery pizza.

**Make lunches** for work and school. Many items can be made in bulk for the week ahead. Don't think you have to do it all. School age children can do this.

**Ban sodas.** Water, iced tea, even Kool-Aid are inexpensive and better for you.

**Eat more unprocessed foods.** A whole potato is less expensive, more filling and better for you than frozen fries or hash browns.

**Make your own bread.** At this writing the average price of a loaf of whole wheat bread is three to four dollars. You can make bread fairly easily by buying a bread making machine at a thrift store or garage sale.

**If you are not the bread baking type,** see if you can find a discount bread store in your area. If you have a freezer you only have to visit once a month.

**Shop Salvage.** Find dented canned goods and outdated toiletries at salvage grocery stores. The date on the package is the "sell by" date. The product will be good for months or years after that date.

**Check the bulk foods aisle**. Measuring out your own oatmeal, beans and flour can save a lot of money.

**Look high and low.** Less expensive brands and generic items are often found on the highest or lowest shelves. Look beyond eye-level and you may find a bargain.

**Veggies:**

**Take a field trip.** Get together with friends and go to an actual field. U-pick farms let you hand-pick your own fruits and vegetables in season. You'll love the prices.

**Can, freeze, dry.** Those same friends can spend a day together preserving your bounty. It's a lot of work, but is so much easier, and even fun, when it's shared.

**Plant a garden.** Even if you only plant one or two things in a patio pot, you'll save money. One tomato plant will produce more tomatoes than a small family can eat during its season.

**Look for Farmers' Markets** in your area. You will almost always get better, fresher produce for a lower price.

**Meats:**

**Find a local butcher.** His prices will be competitive with, sometimes lower than, the supermarket. Your meat will be fresher and of better quality. Butchers often have "package" specials that will include roasts, chops, and burgers for a lower price per pound.

**Buy a cow.** Look into buying a whole steer from a local farmer and having it processed by a local butcher. The last time I did this I got roasts, steaks, stew meat and hamburger that filled my freezer. The cost per pound was about half the retail cost of low-fat hamburger. If a whole steer is too much, you may be able to share it with one or two other families.

## *On Laundry*

**Try to wash only full loads** of clothing. It takes just as much energy to run a small load as a full one.

**Keep it cold.** Unless you tend to get heavy grease on your clothes, cold water does a fine job of keeping your clothes clean.

**Go Outside.** If you have a clothesline, use it. It runs on 100% free solar energy.

**Hang it up.** Indoor clothing racks are great for drying your delicates. They will last longer and look nicer if you don't fry them in the dryer.

Most of your permanent press and knit clothing only needs 10–15 minutes in the dryer to lose their wrinkles. Take them out while they are still damp, hang them up and let them air dry.

**Clean your dryer's lint screen** before every load. A full lint screen cuts down the dryer's efficiency.

**Cut your dryer sheets in half.** You will probably not notice a difference in your clothes.

**Use those half dryer sheets more than once.** You'll be surprised how long they continue to work.

**Make your own dryer sheets.** Buy generic liquid fabric softener and put it in a spray bottle. Spray an old hand towel or T-shirt five or six times. This, too, can be used for quite a few loads before you need to spray it again.

# With Money (Investing)

**Whack the principle.** When you pay off a loan, don't spend the payment amount on new shoes. Add that amount to your payment to the next lender on your list. Every dollar you pay above the required "amount due" goes straight to cutting down your principle (the original amount of the item bought.) That saves you a **lot** of money in interest.

When you get to the happy place of having no more outstanding loans, use the payment money to fatten up your savings.

**Sock the bonus.** Do you get an end-of-the-year bonus? Use 10-20% of the bonus to treat yourself to something fun. Then sock the rest away in savings, preferably in an IRA. You'll thank yourself later!

**Don't overpay the IRS.** The money withheld from your check is being set aside to pay your tax bill. Any extra money withheld comes back to you as a "refund." In effect, you have been loaning the government money all year without receiving any interest for it. If you are getting a big tax refund, decrease your withholding. Put the amount you used to withhold into your savings account and let it earn interest.

**Start long-term savings.** Eventually, you will have enough money in savings that you won't need to have all of it sitting in the bank for an emergency. When you have saved a month of living expenses, it's time to begin a long-term saving and investing plan. Good ideas to begin with:

- See if your employer has a 401(k) plan with matching funds available. Some employers will actually put money in your retirement account, matching whatever you put in, up to a certain percentage of your pay. That's *free money* in your retirement account! You can't afford to pass that up.

- Buy a Certificate of Deposit (CD.) This might be a good strategy if you've never invested before and/or are tempted to spend the cash in your savings account. Cd's are very safe and essentially lock up your money for a period of time. Some will require small up-front amounts and will mature (be available for you to cash out) in a short time. You can get one from your bank.

- Use direct deposit. Your investment money goes right into your 401(k) before you are tempted to spend it on pizza. Your payroll department and/or bank will have the forms to fill out.

- Read a book on investing. You don't even have to buy these books. I'll bet you can check them out at your local library, or borrow them from friends.

**Book Suggestions:**
Investing for Dummies, by Eric Tyson
The Total Money Makeover, by Dave Ramsey

# *Online*

**Don't buy stamps.** Paying bills online will save dollars on postage.

**Don't withdraw.** Do you bank online? Does it make it just a little too convenient to pull money out of savings? Reset your account so you have to go to the bank to withdraw money from savings.

**Look for a discount.** Before you buy anything online check to see if there is an online coupon or discount code available.

**Remember postage.** When buying online, remember to figure in the cost of shipping, including return postage when necessary.

**Compare prices from local sellers.** Often the lower price online turns out to be the same or more when you figure in shipping and handling costs.

**Ask for price matching.** Mention the Internet price to your local merchant. He'll match it if he can. You get your item quickly and support your local businesses: another Win-Win.

## On Your Phone

**Go minimal.** Figure out exactly which features you absolutely must have. Then look for a service plan that will provide what you need for the lowest cost.

**Pay as you go.** Consider using a prepaid phone. Your cost per minute will be higher, but if you can use your phone only for necessary and emergency calls, you can save $50 or more per month.

**Connect with family.** If you are single, see if you can get in on a family plan with your parents or a close friend. Adding a phone to an existing plan is a lot cheaper than buying your own plan.

# While Shopping

## Supermarket Shopping

**Shop with a list.** If it's not on the list, don't buy it.

**Become a bag lady.** Some grocery stores have started charging for bags, especially if you want paper bags. Other stores will actually give you a 5 cent discount for bags you bring in. You have probably been given several eco-shopping bags already. Use them!

**Find the Quick Sale.** Check the clearance, dented-cans shelf and reduced-for-quick-sale areas. Those quick-sale items can go in the freezer which will give you about six months before you need to prepare them.

**Get into coupons.** To really save a lot of money requires learning the tricks as well as how to organize your coupons. Do a web search for "coupons" or "couponing" and you will find many sites willing to educate you. If you find a site that wants you to pay them for the education, move on. There are plenty of blogs that make their money on advertising.

**Record prices.** If you frequent more than one supermarket, keep a record of prices charged for items you buy often. One store will have a lower price on store brand milk, while another charges less for name brand laundry detergent.

## General Shopping

**Hold it.** If you see something you want, but don't need, put it aside. You can usually get a sales person to hold it for you for 24 hours. Think about it for a day or two. You might be surprised how little you care about it once you are not in front of the shiny display.

**Compare prices.** For larger purchases, check prices at three or four different stores. This is so easy to do online. Even if you don't have a computer, you can probably use a computer at your local library.

**Say the seven magic words.** Ask the sales person, in a pleasant voice, "Is that the best you can do?" Usually they will have to ask a manager. You will be surprised how often you can get 10 or 15 percent off the price. (Just remember to pay that 15% to your savings account.)

**Get the pre-sale.** Always ask if the item might be going on sale soon. Very often the sales person can hold the item for you, or even give you the sale price early.

**Resist the "what if?"** Don't buy an item just because it is on sale and you might need it later. Another sale will come along when you need to buy.

**Shop seasonally.** When possible, plan your spending for the time of year the item you need will be on sale. For example, underwear and linens go on sale in January. (See Resources for a list.)

**Shop the back of the store.** When you do go shopping in a retail store (it's okay, it happens to the best of us,) move right past the merchandise at the front of the store. Keep going to the back where the clearance racks dwell. You'll find good stuff at much lower prices.

# On Utilities

### Heating Costs

According to Home Energy Saver (hes.lbl.gov) heating your home eats up 31% of your home energy costs. It is the single largest energy eater in your home. Start with the easiest and least expensive fixes.

**Turn down the thermostat** and wear a sweater, or even two. Wear wool socks and slippers in the house.

**Get dressed for bed.** Cold at night? Wear socks and a hat to bed. Remember Clement Moore's poem, "The Night Before Christmas?" There was a good reason for, "Mama in her kerchief and I in my cap."

**Get down.** One down comforter will keep you cozier than six regular blankets. Yes, they are expensive. But you may be able to turn your thermostat lower than you ever have before. Do your research (Google "how to buy a down comforter") and buy the best one you can afford. Just don't break my heart by paying retail.

**Check your windows and doors** for air leaks. Weather-stripping is an easy Do-It-Yourself project and will save a lot of heat energy.

**Use storm windows** if your windows are old. If you don't have storm windows, buy a plastic storm window kit at the hardware store. They make a difference. A poor man's insulated window can be made with bubble wrap.

Cut the bubble wrap to the size of the window. Use a spray bottle or a sponge to put a thin film of water on the inside of the window. Then press the bubble wrap to the window. This actually works and you can always pull the blinds when company arrives!

**Weatherize your electrical outlets.** On a cold day, put your hand in front of an outlet on an exterior wall. If you feel chilly air, you can fix this pretty cheaply. The hardware store has outlet insulators, little sheets of insulating material cut to fit perfectly behind the outlet plate. Install those *and* child safety plugs in any outlets that aren't being used.

**Copy Great Grandma's winter routine** of changing from frilly summer curtains to heavy winter drapes. Putting heavy fabric in front of the draft helps keep the warm air in and the cold air out.

**Look into new windows.** Insulated windows, that is. If you plan to stay in your house for five to ten years it's worth the investment. Make sure you are getting high quality, low-E windows.

**Tackle a big job.** More expensive fixes include insulating walls, attic and your crawlspace. These may be jobs you can do yourself with a little help from the local library or YouTube.com.

**Get with the program.** If you are likely to forget to turn down the thermostat when you leave the house or go to bed, you might want to invest in a programmable thermostat. It will remember for you that no one is home between 8 a.m. and 5:30 p.m. on weekdays. Look for one with multiple settings so you don't find yourself freezing on the weekends.

**Be more efficient.** You might want to look into an updated, more efficient furnace. Again, look into the amount of savings you can expect per year versus the number of years you expect to stay in the house.

## Appliances

**Unplug appliances** when you aren't using them.

**Cut the cable.** How much cable TV do you really watch? Can you get by on free network TV? Believe it or not, there are people who survive without cable.

**Check the label.** If you need a new appliance, check for an Energy Star label. This tells you that your new dryer, refrigerator or computer uses 20%-30% less energy than the federal government requires. That's good for your pocket book.

**Soften up.** If you live in a hard water area, consider installing a water softener. It is not inexpensive, but over time it can save having to replace everything from your dishwasher to your water pipes. Get advice from a plumber as to how important this is in your area.

## Hot Water

Heating your water eats up about 12% of your energy money. So think about ways to use less of it.

**Turn it down.** You can turn the thermostat on your electric water heater down to 120°. That's plenty warm for cleaning up the kiddos. Remember, your dishwasher has its own heating element, so no need to worry about germs there.

**Cold water wash.** Most of your clothes can be washed in cold water and still come clean. So do that.

**Insulate your hot water heater.** You can get a water heater jacket at your local home store or online. This makes a lot of sense if your hot water heater is in your garage. But it works for an inside water heater too. Why air condition your hot water heater?

**Go low flow.** Today's low-flow shower heads are really very good. You'll save hot water without sacrificing a great shower.

**Cooling**

**Fans are your friend.** An indoor breeze helps you feel about 4° cooler so you can turn up the thermostat and use the air conditioner less. Fans cool people, not the air. So turn them off when no one is in the room.

**Plant deciduous trees** on the west and south sides of your house. They will shade the areas that get the most direct sunlight, but won't block the sun's rays in the winter.

**Make shade.** An awning or porch, even a bamboo shade hung a few feet in front of the window, will create a shade buffer in front of your windows.

**Use wind power.** Figure out which way the winds usually blow and open the windows that will allow the breeze to flow through the house. Depending on where you live, this may be all the air conditioning you need. Or, it might be enough cooling for night time.

# Resources

| Who | What |
| --- | --- |
| DAVERAMSEY.COM | Financial Education |
| Mint.com | Online Money Management Tools |
| MyMoney.gov | Free educational resources from the U.S. government |
| MSN.MONEY | Compare Credit Card Features |
| CarTalk.com | Fun way to learn about cars. Helpful if you are in the market for a new or used car. |
| Wisebread.com/buying-calendar | A list detailing what time of year to find sales on specific items. |
| MarthaStewart.com | Answers to all your home, clothing and garden questions. |
| Mr.GoodwillHunting.com and ApartmentTherapy.com | Home Design and fashion on a skinny budget. |

# About the Author

Marilyn Woodard draws on 30 years of experience, education & research, to advise the next generation on home matters like marriage, family, educating children, interior design, and handling your money.

If you are interested in hearing more from Marilyn, please visit her website, **Miz Woody's Place.**

**www.MizWoodysPlace.com**

# Photo Credits

Guitar Woman by Rebecca Pollard
http://www.flickr.com/photos/34396501@N00/58694179/

Calculator by 401K
http://www.flickr.com/photos/68751915@N05/673619409
9/

Bundled Woman by justin
http://www.flickr.com/photos/justin/2097139259/sizes/o/in
/photostream/

Made in the USA
Middletown, DE
08 December 2022